KELMSCOTT MANOR

AN ILLUSTRATED GUIDE

THE SOCIETY OF ANTIQUARIES OF LONDON 2(

Kelmscott lies in the south-west corner of Oxfordshire between Lechlade and Faringdon.

For times of opening please telephone: 01367 252486 or visit www.kelmscottmanor.co.uk

Kelmscott Manor
Kelmscott
Lechlade
Glos GL7 3HJ

ISBN 0-85431-269-2
Designed by Visible Edge, London
Printed by B·A·S Printers Ltd, Salisbury, Wiltshire

CONTENTS

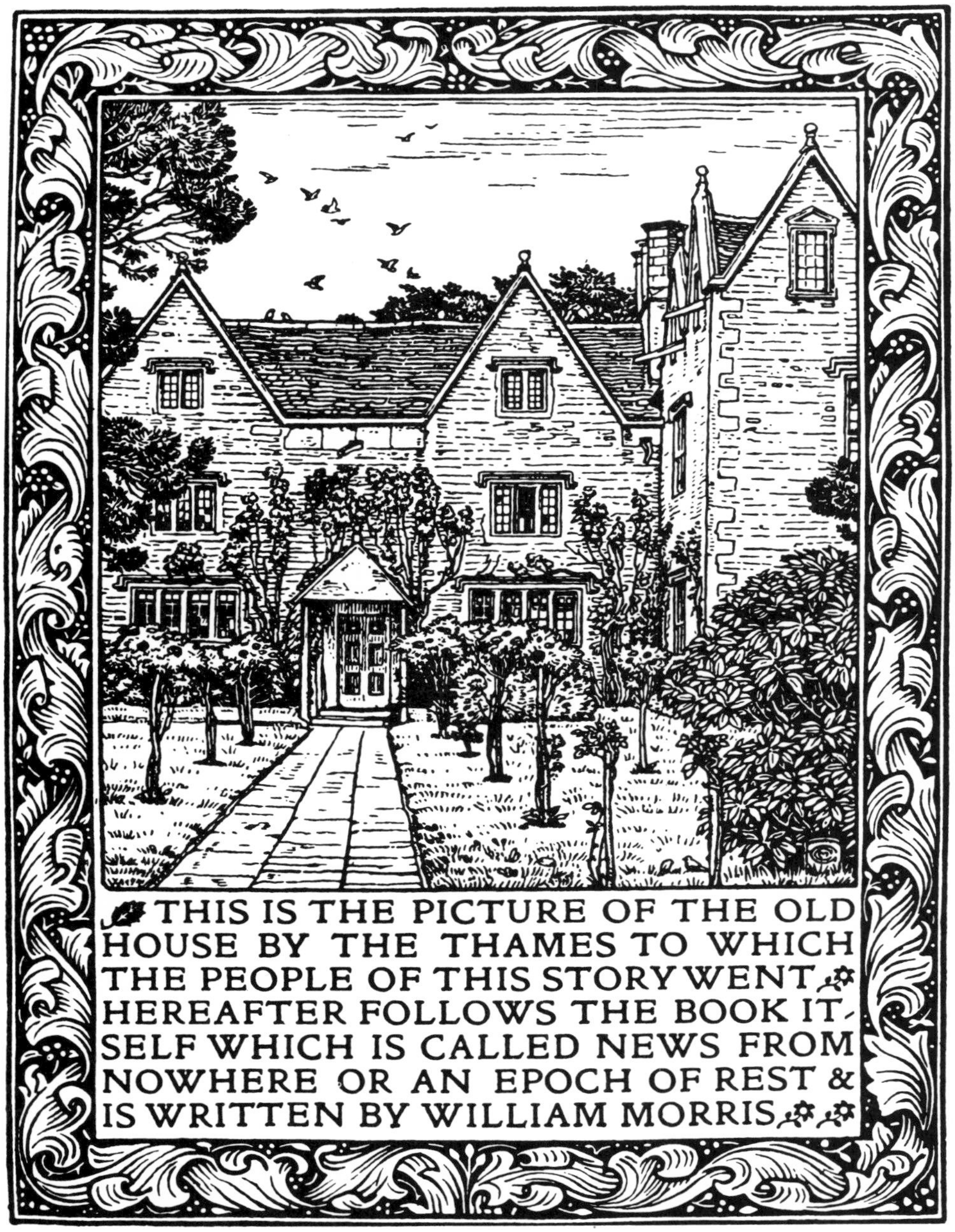

1

Frontispiece of News from Nowhere (Kelmscott Press, 1892), drawn by C. M. Gere, with border designed by Morris, cut by W. H. Hooper

THIS IS THE PICTURE OF THE OLD HOUSE BY THE THAMES TO WHICH THE PEOPLE OF THIS STORY WENT. HEREAFTER FOLLOWS THE BOOK IT-SELF WHICH IS CALLED NEWS FROM NOWHERE OR AN EPOCH OF REST & IS WRITTEN BY WILLIAM MORRIS

I INTRODUCTION

'I have been looking for a house for the wife and kids, and whither do you think my eye is turned now? Kelmscott, a little village about two miles above Radcot Bridge – a heaven on earth; an old stone Elizabethan house like Water Eaton, and such a garden! close down on the river, a boat house and all things handy. I am going down there again with Rossetti and my wife: Rossetti because he thinks of sharing it with us if the thing looks likely...'

So wrote William Morris to C. J. Faulkner on 17 May, 1871 and, in 1895, the year before he died, Morris wrote an essay called 'Gossip about an Old House on the Upper Thames';

> You enter through a door in a high impointed stone wall, having passed by first a pretty characteristic cottage with its baking oven much *en evidence*, and next a shed with a high pitched roof. Entering the door in the wall you go up a flagged path through a front garden to the porch, which is a modern but harmless addition in wood. The house from this side is a lowish three storied one with the beautiful stone slates of the district, the most lovely covering which a roof can have, especially when, as here and in all the traditional old houses of the countryside, they are 'sized down'; the smaller ones to the top and the bigger ones toward the eaves, which gives one the same sort of pleasure in their orderly beauty as a fish's scales or a bird's feathers... The garden, divided by old clipped yew hedges, is quite unaffected and very pleasant, and looks in fact as if it were part of the house, yet at least the clothes of it: which I think ought to be the aim of the layer-out of a garden.

These two quotations enable us to understand the attraction of Kelmscott for Morris. His delight in discovering it can be felt by visitors today. It is the most evocative of all the houses associated with Morris. The house and its principal contents were preserved after his death by his younger daughter, May, from whom it has passed to the Society of Antiquaries.

II KELMSCOTT AND THE MORRIS FAMILY

Kelmscott Manor – 'an old house which my sister and I consider the only house in England worth inhabiting!' according to May Morris – always held a special place in the affections of the Morris family, as an ideal house and ideal home.

In part this was because it was a holiday home, habitable only in summer owing to lack of heating and winter floods, and hence a place of pleasure, leisure, escape. When Morris began 'looking for a house for the wife and kids' in estate agents' catalogues, the family were living in Queen Square, central London, on the same premises as the workshops of the firm, Morris, Marshall, Faulkner & Co., with no garden but the soot-blackened communal Square. Clean air was considered essential for health; Morris's wife Janey had been ill and the two girls were not strong; seaside lodgings or a house in the country was the usual prescription.

But this concealed another, less advertised motive. In 1871, William and Jane Morris had been married for 12 years. Their daughters Jenny and May were aged ten and nine. For some time, an *amitié amoureuse* had been developing between Jane and Dante Gabriel Rossetti, painter, poet and partner in the Firm. Neither separation nor divorce was possible without scandal and social ostracism. A shared house deep in the country – and Kelmscott is certainly off the beaten track – offered a solution, out of the reach of gossip. A joint lease was arranged between Morris and Rossetti.

Morris wrote about such a place the following year in his unfinished novel, describing

"a village not so very far from London, yet in a country out of the tracks of the busiest people... with a remote and unchanging air about it, that put it beyond dullness and made the commonplace people, who wore away their monotonous and thoughtless lives there seem to the dreamy wanderer through the streets as if they must deal with a different code of right and wrong, different ways of hope and fear and pleasure and pain than him..."

With a lifelong passion for old buildings, Morris had learned to love the villages around Oxford while at the University with Edward Burne-Jones, his close friend and colleague. Here too he had met Oxford-born Philip Webb, architect and partner in the Firm. As for Janey, when she first came to Kelmscott she described the countryside, though rather flat, as 'all delightful and home-like', for both her parents had been born in nearby villages –

her mother at Alvescot and her father at Stanton Harcourt – before moving to work in Oxford, where Jane was born and lived until her marriage.

Discovered by Rossetti while he and his companions were painting Knights of the Round Table on the high-coved ceiling of the University debating chamber, Jane Burden accepted Morris's proposal in 1858. She was only 18, a stableman's daughter; Morris was 24, with a large unearned income.

2
William Morris aged about 53

Their first home was Red House in Kent, designed by Philip Webb, where the idea of Morris and Co. was born. During the 1860s Morris made his name not as a designer but as a poet, author of *The Life and Death of Jason* and *The Earthly Paradise*. Jane and her sister Elizabeth supervised the embroidery side of the Firm, and also undertook much of the needlework themselves. Bessie Burden later became an instructor at the Royal School of Needlework and adviser to schools in the London area.

Morris brought Jane and the girls to Kelmscott in June 1871 and then left for Iceland. Rossetti had already moved in. It was, Morris told his mother, 'the "loveliest haunt of ancient peace" that can well be imagined', surrounded by thatched farm buildings, 'which looked settled down into a purring state of comfort, but seem (as Janey said the other day) as if you were to stroke them, they would move'.

Rossetti set up his painting studio in the Tapestry Room. There is no conclusive evidence of the degree of intimacy between Janey and himself, but their correspondence suggests they were very much in love and happy to be together all summer – together too, of course, with the girls, a governess and several servants. Their affair, if that's what it was, was very discreet. Morris was stoical and generous. 'Please dear Janey, be happy', he wrote on his departure.

Several of Rossetti's poems celebrate Kelmscott in thinly disguised form:

Between Holmscote and Hurstcote
    The river reaches wind,
The whispering trees accept the breeze,
    The ripple's cool and kind
With love low-whispered 'twixt the shores
    With rippling laughter gay,
With white arms bare to ply the oars,
    On last year's first of May.

3
D. G. Rossetti. Studio portrait by W&D Downey, London 1862

He also painted Jane in the *Water-Willow* image, a copy of which hangs in the bedroom she occupied. 'It bothered me to have house and church and boathouse all brought together when they were really in different directions,' recalled May, of the picture's subsidiary motifs; 'I confided to my mother my doubts as to the morality of this and demanded an explanation. But the child's "that isn't how things really are!" can't be met by explanation'.

Jane set about decorating and renovating. 'I am getting the fireplace set straight in the dining room, the one with the broken mantelshelf,' she wrote to Webb, 'and I think it would look well with tiles. Would you be so kind as to see about these at Queen Square for me? Six dozen would be enough, 5-inch ones... two rows on each side and a single row along the top, the rest for the inside of the fireplace which will be an open one. Will they look best of various patterns or all alike? They must be blue. The mantelpiece is stone I find so I am making the masons scrape off the former drab paint. The next thing to be thought of is the grate...'

Jenny and May loved the Manor. They learnt to handle the heavy punt on the river backwaters and clambered over the roofs (where May once stuck astride the highest ridge until long ladders were brought from the farm). From Iceland their father brought a pony named Mouse who grew plump on the rich paddock grass. It was a perfect holiday home – complete with a tradition that the Manor was haunted by the ghost of a long ago resident.

In 1872 Rossetti suffered a major mental collapse, afflicted with delusions, voices, irrational suspicion. From autumn of that year until

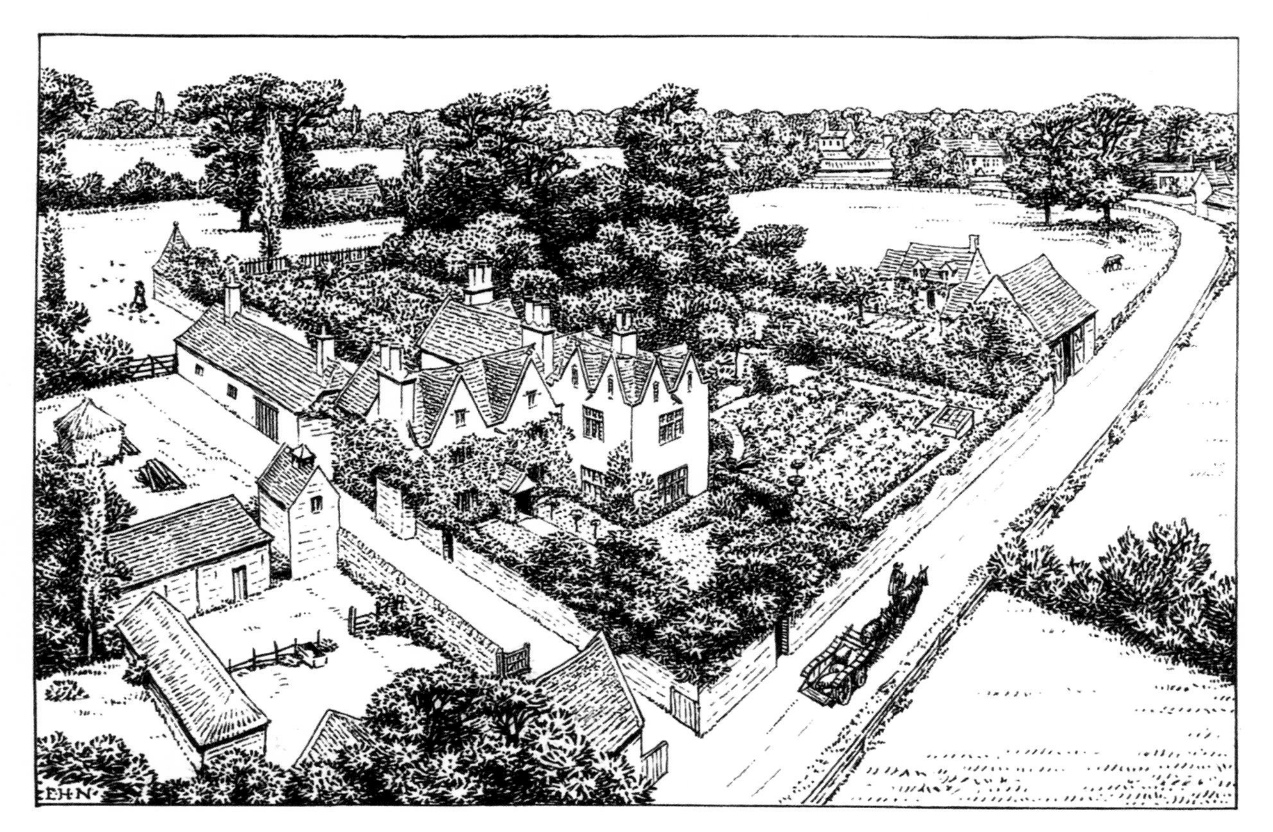

4
Drawing of Kelmscott Manor and Gardens by E. H. New

summer 1874 he lived at Kelmscott in virtual seclusion, Janey joining him for a few summer weeks. Eventually paranoia and unpredictable behaviour drove him back to London, but not before his mother and sister Christina had been to visit. 'A lovely homely house,' Christina wrote later, 'close to the river with its endless delights of rushes, lilies and other beauties... and not only a flower garden but strawberries and raspberries and other treats'.

Earlier in the year, Morris had determined on relinquishing his share of the lease, feeling that Rossetti was never likely to leave and moreover had 'all sorts of ways so unsympathetic with the sweet simple old place' since his breakdown. Once Rossetti had departed, however, Morris renewed the tenancy. From 1874 the Manor became the family's second home, nominally co-tenanted by F. S. Ellis, Morris's publisher, who shared his passion for coarse fishing, but the family's to all intents and purposes. One of Jane's last acts was to purchase the property, to secure it for her daughters.

Kelmscott became even more valuable and valued after 1875 when Jenny developed epilepsy, in due course becoming permanently disabled by mental impairment. To the end of her long life, it remained her greatest pleasure to be at Kelmscott. Morris, increasingly busy with his work for the restructured Firm, and then with his commitment to the Socialist cause was able to snatch only the odd weekend or week in the country. Sometimes he came by himself, out of season, savouring the atmosphere. 'I'm sitting now [at] ten p.m. in the tapestry room, the moon rising red through the east wind haze, and a cow lowing over the fields,' he wrote in 1879. I have been feeling chastened by many thoughts and the beauty and quietness of the surroundings...'

Early in 1877 he came for a couple of days in the 'coldest and wildest' weather, with drifting snow showers and frost. Within a week he was writing to the press with ideas of setting up a committee to save old buildings – 'for the purpose of watching over and protecting those relics which, scanty as they are now become, are still wonderful treasures in this age of the world'. The consequent Society for the Protection of Ancient Buildings would in due course rescue many other old houses like those at Kelmscott.

Kelmscott also became the symbol and standard of the quality of life he wished everyone to enjoy. As he wrote to Georgiana Burne-Jones in 1880, 'I have more than ever at my heart the importance for people of living in beautiful places; I mean the sort of beauty which would be attainable by all, if people could but begin to long for it.' Almost more important than the attainment of beauty and peace was the desire for it, the refusal to be satisfied with less.

Kelmscott is the culmination of Morris's Utopian romance *News from Nowhere*, in which the narrator journeys with his companion up the Thames to join in the haymaking:

> We crossed the road and again almost without my will my hand raised the latch of a door in the wall, and we stood presently on a stone path which led up to the old house... My companion gave a sign of pleased surprise and enjoyment; nor did I wonder, for the garden between the wall and the house was redolent of the June flowers, and the roses were rolling over one another with that delicious superabundance which at first sight takes away all thought from the beholder save that of beauty. The blackbirds were singing their loudest, the doves were cooing on the roof-ridge, the rooks in the high elm trees beyond were garrulous among the young leaves, and the swifts wheeled whining about the gables. And the house itself was a fit guardian for all the beauty of this heart of summer.

5
Family group at Kelmscott in the years after Morris's death: May, her mother, Jenny and Jenny's nurse-companion

Morris died in October 1896, at Kelmscott House, Hammersmith, at the other end of the Thames and named after the Manor as is if to show where his real home lay. And it is at Kelmscott that he lies buried, beside the small church. The cortege arrived at Lechlade by rail, on a wet and windy day, with the low-lying meadows already under flood waters. 'Four countrymen in moleskins carried the unpolished oak coffin decorated with bay wreaths to an open hay cart with yellow body and bright wheels wreathed in vine leaves, strewn with willow boughs and carpeted with moss', recorded the local paper. Janey, looking pale and shaken, was escorted by Burne-Jones and followed by her daughters and in-laws, Morris's brothers and sisters. At the church, a small group of villagers waited with Rev. Fulford Adams, rector of Faringdon and college friend of Morris. The bell rang tinnily; the rain dripped from the trees as if in melancholy sympathy with the funeral. Inside, the church was decorated for harvest festival, almost as Morris had envisioned it as the setting for the haymaking supper at the end of *News from Nowhere.* Outside, his coffin was lowered into the ground, in due course to be joined by those of his wife and daughters.

After Morris's death, Jane continued to live at Kelmscott in the summers, always reluctant to shut the house up for the winter. One of her first thoughts as a widow was to build a memorial to her husband that would benefit the village. One idea was a reading room, but eventually Jane asked Philip Webb to design a pair of cottages on land close to the Manor, one of which was to house a schoolteacher, for she was also concerned with the village children's educational opportunities. 'Almost the very first building I set up was for you,' Webb replied, with reference to Red House, 'and the very last, if I can so make it, will also be for you.' And he added: 'Even if you had not said so, I know you look on your work of the cottages as the *real* memorial in connection with the love of our "old man" for so many years with Kelmscott...'

Jane died early in 1914, having purchased the Manor. May retained her house in Hammersmith, but during World War I spent a good deal of time at Kelmscott, where she commissioned Ernest Gimson, a leading Arts and Crafts architect and Morris follower, then living in the Cotswolds, to design a second pair of cottages, in memory of her mother. She also did her best to support and improve village life. 'There was never enough cottages in the village, and they let them fall down', recalled one resident. 'This one was condemned, they was going to pull it down; Miss Morris bought it and had it put to rights. It's four cottages now – she said we wasn't never to be turned out of them!' May was also involved in setting up the Kelmscott Women's Institute, and the inaugural meeting was held at the Manor in June 1916, with a demonstration of bottling fruit, a talk on War Loans and a display of country dancing by the village children.

6
Memorial Cottages
Designed by Philip Webb

Later in the war May offered accommodation to Mary Frances Lobb, who had come to Kelmscott as a land girl. Large and burly, usually clad in tweeds and breeches, Miss Lobb soon became a fixture, regarded with some amusement by visitors. But one student interviewed by May as a prospective school mistress had a warm memory of being fetched from the station in the pony and trap driven by a cheerful Miss Lobb, discoursing in a loud voice: 'She came from the West Country during the war and never wanted to leave. She loves ponies, the land, the life. I catch aslant her shining eyes, red cheeks, enthusiasm.'

'There will assuredly sooner or later be raised some memorial to my father in Kelmscott, and I want such a memorial to be raised in the lifetime of all of us: and I want it to take the shape of the little hall that in pre-war days we were to have built in the family,' wrote May in 1918, adding that she also wanted the residents of Kelmscott to have a share in raising this memorial to Morris, 'who was their friend and champion' and who believed that any hope for the art of England lay in the reawakened life of ordinary people. Whenever visitors made a pilgrimage to Kelmscott to see the house William Morris had loved, she asked for donations and in his centenary year of 1934 was at last able to raise the hall, at the far end of the village, that had been designed by Gimson. The opening ceremony was performed by Bernard Shaw, at the height of his fame as a dramatist, and the hall was packed so full that an unexpected visitor, Prime Minister Ramsay Macdonald, was unable to get in. Both men had been admirers of Morris in his Socialist years.

7
May and Miss Lobb on holiday in the mountains in the 1930s

Thus May was able to realise her dream of raising a memorial that would benefit the people of Kelmscott. In her last years she lived permanently at the manor, where she died in 1938, having also provided him with another memorial in the shape of his *Collected Works* in 24 volumes, with two supplementary volumes of political papers and essays.

Several of Morris's essays draw on the environment at Kelmscott, as part of his vision of regeneration. As he wrote in 1889:

> Midsummer in the country : here you may walk between the fields and hedges that are as it were one huge nosegay for you, redolent of bean-flowers and clover and sweet hay and elder-blossom. The cottage gardens are bright with flowers, the cottages themselves mostly models of architecture in their way... Man in the past, nature in the present, seem to be bent on pleasing you and making all things delightful to your senses; even the burning dirty road has a look of luxury as you lie on the strip of roadside green, and listen to the blackbirds singing, surely for your benefit, and, I was going to say, as if they were paid to do it, but I was wrong, for as it is they seem to be doing their best.

III THE MANOR EXTERIOR AND INTERIOR

The qualities in Kelmscott Manor, which appealed to William Morris, are those that still appeal today. Its setting remains very much as it was when he found it; the house is built and roofed with the local stone, the layout is a traditional one, and its architectural details are those long employed by the country mason. Even without its associations with Morris, the house would be of considerable interest: it is a fine example of the house of prosperous, seventeenth century yeoman farmers and lesser gentry, and its history since Morris occupied it has led to its preservation largely in accordance with principles that he – as co-founder of the Society for the Protection of Ancient Buildings – would have approved.

The earlier part of the house was probably built by Thomas Turner, a prosperous yeoman farmer who died in 1610. His house remains in all its essentials. Entrance is into a passage divided off from the hall by a wooden screen; to the left of the front door (south – not shown to the public) was the kitchen, and beyond the hall (north) was a parlour. To the rear are two wings, with a second parlour in the northern wing and further service rooms in the southern. At the north end of the house the original, principal stair leads to the upper floors; at the southern end is a narrow service stair in the angle by the kitchen fireplace. The original roof timbers largely survive; the principal of these are of elm, the characteristic tree of the region until the 1970s.

The Turner family owned property in the nearby villages of Broadwell and Filkins as well as in Kelmscott, and it is uncertain who was living in the house following the death of Thomas Turner I. But in the 1660s it was occupied by another Thomas Turner, described at the time as 'gentleman' and whose wealth and status prompted him to build a new wing at the north east of the house. Outside, the gable windows are dignified with simple, classical, pedimented surrounds – ornament that can be paralleled elsewhere in the area in houses of a similar class and date. Inside, the two rooms in this new wing are larger and grander than those in the old house, and the stone fireplaces have the coat of arms that was granted to Thomas Turner II in 1665.

Both of these rooms have bays giving off them on their north side; the first floor bay, now open to the tapestry room, may originally have been a separate dressing room or powder closet. Other work was carried out at the same time: the parlour in the north west wing was given a new fireplace, a bay was added to it looking over the garden (originally heated, and perhaps serving

8

The east front, showing the seventeenth-century house with the addition of about 1665-1675 on the right

9

The main staircase

as a little study), and the gables of the older part of the house were heightened to enhance its overall appearance.

However, the present decoration of the two rooms in Thomas Turner II's new wing is largely of the early eighteenth century, probably carried out for George Turner who died in 1734. On the ground floor the parlour has simple panelling, painted white in Morris's time and probably so painted originally. The first floor room is hung with seventeenth century tapestry, cut about to fit and probably installed at the same time as the panelling below; it is not known where it came from. At the time of George Turner's death the house seems to have been subdivided, with the southern part of the house leased to a tenant. This may have been the occasion for other changes, including the creation of an entrance hall for George Turner's use at the centre of the north front of the house.

10

View from the Tapestry Room window

Thereafter, although the Turner family retained ownership of the house until 1913, they seem seldom to have lived there and generally rented or leased it out; this too has been a reason for its preservation. William, Janey and May Morris did little to it; they installed an inside toilet (though water had still to be pumped into a tank in the roof); they re-opened a window in the china closet that had at some time been blocked, laid flagstones on the hall floor, and lined the fireplaces with the tiles that are there now.

When May Morris died and the house passed to Oxford University, the house was in poor condition. Repairs and some modernisation were needed if a tenant was to be found, work that was undertaken in 1939-40 under the supervision of the architect T. G. Davidson. Nevertheless, when the house passed to the Society of Antiquaries in 1962 (see Epilogue) much still had to be done if it was to be shown regularly to the public. Much woodwork had to be renewed in the roof, and walls, chimneys and floors were stabilised. A late fireplace surround was removed in the hall, revealing the original opening of c. 1600, and parts of a glazed partition that in Morris's time had formed an enclosure in the north hall and had been moved elsewhere by Davidson were re-used in the north hall to make a draught screen. This work, done under Peter Locke of Donald Insall, Associates, was widely recognised at the time for the care and sensitivity with which it was carried out.

IV TOUR OF THE HOUSE

The house is not arranged exactly as Morris knew it. It now contains several layers of possessions. As a rented holiday place, it contained little of his furniture. Some of the objects associated with the Turner family still survive such as the tapestries in the Tapestry Room. There are also a number of objects, mainly rather exotic, collected by Rossetti. Most of the present contents were brought from Kelmscott House in Hammersmith after Morris's death. These include some of the objects designed for Red House near Bexley in Kent. This was designed for William and Janey by Philip Webb in 1859, was their home from 1860 to 1865, and is now owned by the National Trust, and open to the public. May Morris continued to possess a London house, No. 8 Hammersmith Terrace, which was taken initially on her marriage with Henry Halliday Sparling in 1890. She left London in 1923. Four at least of the Rossetti portraits and the Dürer woodcuts came from No. 8. Much of the evidence for provenance comes from the inventory attached to May's will of 1929. More recently there have been many new gifts of objects associated with and related to William Morris and his family.

THE SCREENS PASSAGE

The dark and narrow screens passage, hung with *Cherwell* velveteen curtains designed in 1887, leads into the Hall. The seventeenth-century oak chest is believed to have been always in the house. The embroidered altar frontal, by May Morris and dating from the late 1920s, contains the quotation 'The heavens declare the Glory of God: and the firmament sheweth his handiwork'.

THE HALL

The Hall is low-ceilinged, and retains the original seventeenth-century fireplace. Two oak chairs and one of the oak tables were already in the house in 1871. The walls are hung with faded hangings of the *Strawberry Thief* chintz, registered 1883, which may have been here since 1896. The embroidery of Penelope, mounted on green serge, is one of a number of embroidered hangings designed by Morris for Red House. On the table are eight tablemats embroidered by May between 1923 and 1933. The original designs are in an exercise book on display in the north east garret (see page p.30-1). The small ebonised occasional chairs of the popular *Sussex* range, retailed by the Morris

11
The Hall

firm from 1866 onwards, cost seven shillings in 1912. In the corner cupboard are several plates and tiles of the second half of the sixteenth century, produced in the region of the north-west Anatolian town of Iznik. The oak buffet was designed by Philip Webb for Red House. On it are examples of glasses by James Powell and Sons, a chafing dish by W. A. S. Benson and bowls from Berne, Switzerland. The etching of Primavera by Botticelli is by F. Zasinski, and dates from the 1890s.

THE NORTH HALL

This is entered from the Hall through a second screens-passage and retains no evidence of a fireplace. The seventeenth-century oak 'screen' of the screens-passage was reinstalled here in 1966 from the first floor. The screen is unusual for two reasons: it appears to have been glazed, and it constitutes a very

12
Cushion cover embroidered by May Morris

13

Queen Guenevere: unfinished embroidered hanging. The design derives from an early drawing of Janey (Burden) by Morris

late example of the medieval screening arrangement. On the left is a hanging embroidery on linen originally made for Red House. It derives from Morris's early sketch of Jane as Guenevere or La Belle Iseult made before their marriage in 1859. It is an unfinished work by Jane and Bessie and the annotation about colouring may be by Jane Morris. The embroidered hangings of dark blue serge and faded wool yarns with daisy patterns attached to the screen were worked on by Jane and friends and family for the principal bedroom at Red House. On the wall on the left is the important Cabbage and Vine tapestry described by May Morris as 'W. M.'s own piece', which was his first attempt at tapestry weaving in 1879.

14
The settle and blue serge Daisy hangings

On the south wall is the settle, of ebonised wood with curved hood and panels decorated with flowers and diapering painted on leather. It was designed by Philip Webb for Red House between 1860 and 1865, and, in describing Red House, May Morris records that, in the dining room, 'the black settle with gilt and painted leather panels, now at Kelmscott, was placed by the hospitable fireplace.' The eighteenth-century Burmese gilded and ebonised chest belonged to Rossetti as did the satinised Pembroke table of c. 1800. Framed on the walls are eleven charcoal drawings of the 'Signs of the Zodiac' by Edward Burne-Jones, which are the original sketches for the small painted figures on the panelling of the 'Green Dining Room' in the Victoria and Albert Museum (Aries is missing). This was one of the first important secular works of Morris and Co. in 1866-7. Hanging on the door is William Morris's overcoat. The two brass candlesticks were designed by W. A. S. Benson c. 1890. The large round dish in ruby lustre was designed by William de Morgan during his Chelsea period 1872-82. The swan is designed by Walter Crane, and made by Maw and Co in 1889.

Beyond is the Panelled Room and beside the doorway to it is another Red House embroidered figure, mounted on brown velvet, of St. Catharine standing beside a tree. This was worked in brick stitch by Jane around 1860. Opposite are two full-size designs around 1912-4, one in line, the other colour, for the *millefleurs* tapestry in the next room.

THE PANELLED ROOM

This was the drawing room and it has a higher ceiling and a fine late seventeenth-century stone fireplace with swags and a shield painted with the Turner arms. These were – argent a cross azure in each quarter a millrind azure with a crest of a lion passant. The panelling above the fireplace is late seventeenth century and the rest of the panelling is either of that date or early eighteenth century. The room is, and evidently always has been, painted entirely white. It may have influenced, through Webb and the Morris firm, the late nineteenth and early twentieth-century fashion for white interiors. Tattered remains of curtains found in the room in 1964 were also white, and the modern

15
The Panelled Room, with an original fireplace of about 1670 and eighteenth-century panelling

16

The 'Blue silk Dress'.

Rossetti's portrait of Janey Morris aged 26

linen replacements provide a similar effect. The tiles in the fireplace were made by an unidentified Dutch tileworks, and were influenced by Iznik designs.

Here, and in the adjoining Closet, are those pictures which are visual evidence of the close friendship of Rossetti with the Morris family, and in particular with Janey, in whom the sensuous and the mystic seemed to combine to provide him with his ideal model. They include four drawings and one painting of her by Rossetti completed when she was 17, 21, 30 and 34 years of age. She was born in 1840. The earliest, in the closet, is the first known portrait of Jane Burden. The two drawings of her aged 21 were studies for the Virgin in Rossetti's altar-piece for Llandaff Cathedral, Wales. The altarpiece was begun in 1858 and finished in 1864. May Morris considered these drawings as 'particularly valuable as portraiture in their freedom from type-exaggeration'. The outstanding portrait, the *Blue Silk Dress*, Rossetti's oil painting of her, may have been begun as early as 1865 (when she was 25) and was finished in 1868. Letters from Rossetti to Jane Morris indicate that she made the sumptuous blue silk dress herself. The Latin couplet on the picture

> 'Conjuge clara poeta, et praeclarissima vultu,
> Denique pictura clara sit illa mea'

may be translated 'Famed for her poet husband, and of surpassing fame for her beauty, now let her win lasting fame by my painting', which echoes the last line of Rossetti's passionate sonnet The Portrait, 'They that would look on her must come to me', written in the same year, 1868. Janey Morris's mysterious beauty fascinated Rossetti and others throughout her life and was never more strongly revealed than in this portrait. The last drawing of 12 August 1870 shows Janey reclining whole length on a sofa with eyes looking down.

17
Janey Morris aged 21. Rossetti's sketch for the Virgin in his altar-piece for Llandaff Cathedral

Relics of Rossetti's sojourn at Kelmscott are his two delightful coloured chalk drawings of Jenny and May, dated 1871, made when they were 10 and 9 respectively. The frames were designed by Rossetti. A small undated oil painting, of the two girls at Naworth Castle, Cumberland, the home of the Hon. George Howard, who painted it in oils around 1870, hangs on the fireplace wall.

Over the fireplace is a painting by Peter Breughel the younger signed and dated 1632. May Morris called it the 'Tulip Garden' but it derives from the elder Breughel's drawing of *Spring* now in the Albertina in Vienna. The painting is reversed from the original and is probably copied from Pieter van de Heyden's engraving of the drawing. Three easy chairs, upholstered in *Peacock and Dragon*, are typical of those retailed by Morris and Co from the late nineteenth-century. The black and gilded occasional armchair was made to Webb's design, and exhibited by Morris, Marshall, Faulkner, and Company in the Medieval Court at the 1862 International Exhibition in London. The light fitting in the centre of the room is an electrolier by W. A. S Benson.

18
Soft pastel drawings by Rossetti of Jenny (aged 10) and May (aged 9) (1871)

The circular table was designed by G. Jack for the firm c. 1890. The mid eighteenth-century lacquered corner cupboards, belonged to Rossetti. The pair of candle branches were designed by W. A. S. Benson c. 1890. Hanging by the door is a *millefleurs* tapestry of Morris and Co. designed by J. H. Dearle, woven at Merton Abbey in the early 1920s.

In the Closet there is an ebonised "whatnot", part of a series of furniture designed by Webb and made by Morris, Marshall, Faulkner and Co. c. 1860. The blue wallpaper is a modern printing of *Sunflower* designed by Morris in 1879 and the blue and white china on the white-painted display shelving designed by Philip Webb aptly demonstrate Walter Crane's assessment of the change in Victorian interior decoration and furnishing accomplished by Morris and Co. Crane wrote in 1897 'plain white or green paint for interior woodwork drove graining and marbling to the public-house; blue and white Nankin, Delft or *Grès de Flandres* routed Dresden and Sèvres from the cabinet...'. The collection of blue and white china belonged to Morris and is Chinese, Japanese, and Dutch dating from the eighteenth to nineteenth centuries. Much German stoneware (Grès de Flandres ware) survives in the house, particularly in the Green Room.

THE GREEN ROOM

This is hung round with *Kennet* chintz designed by Morris in 1883. Two printing blocks for *Kennet* are displayed in this room. The late seventeenth-century fireplace has a plain armorial cartouche. The tiles in the fireplace are all William Morris designs. *Artichoke* and *Swan* were put in during 1873. *Sunflower* and *Snakeshead* were much later (1960s) replacements for damaged and broken tiles.

The large round table in medieval taste was designed by Philip Webb about 1860 for Red House and is described by May Morris as 'the first made', presumably for the Morris firm. The seventeenth-century oak chair with a book-box in the seat was known as Jenny's chair. There is an Italian sixteenth-century chest with pokerwork decoration, and three chests associated with the Turner family.

The covers of the chair and sofa are made up of fragments of the heavy double-weave wool fabric *Bird*, in blue, designed by Morris in 1878. This was the textile first used for wall hanging in the dining room of Kelmscott House. In the bay beside the far window is an embroidered wool hanging of prime importance. Known as the *If I can* embroidery (see p.33), it represents Morris's first experiments in about 1857 to produce a textile. It was made to furnish his first lodgings at London in Red Lion Square. It was embroidered both by him and his maid, 'Red Lion Mary' (Mary Nicholson).

The tiles depicting heroines from Chaucer's 'Legend of Goode Wimmen' (sic) were designed by Edward Burne-Jones and were early products of Morris, Marshall, Faulkner and Co. The Icelandic needle case, dated 1844, was given to May Morris on one of her visits to Iceland in the 1920s. The brass dishes here and in other rooms were made in Augsburg in the sixteenth century.

19

Printing blocks for 'Kennet'

20

The Green Room

STAIRS

Proceeding up the seventeenth-century stairs, on the left is a tapestry of Samson slaying the lion, one of the series of mid seventeenth-century Brussels or Antwerp tapestries of the Life of Samson which Morris found in the house in 1871. On the opposite wall is a pair of late seventeenth-century oil paintings left by Rossetti of scenes in a Spanish town, probably Sahagun on the pilgrimage route to Compostella. They are in early composition frames. The mid eighteenth-century 'tavern' clock by Godfrye Poy was given to Rossetti. The copper candlesticks were designed by Webb c. 1860 for Red House. The light fittings were designed by W. A. S. Benson. On the landing at the top of the stairs, is displayed Morris's ink working drawing, done in December 1895, for the stamped pigskin bindings of the Kelmscott Chaucer. The great Kelmscott Chaucer was begun in 1894 and by an immense effort completed in 1896, the first copy being placed in Morris's hands three months before his death.

21
Copy of Rossetti's Water-Willow with Janey's jewel casket

MRS MORRIS'S BEDROOM

Mrs. Morris's Room, to the right, is sited above the Green room and faces west. The walls are covered with a modern printing of *Willow Boughs* designed by Morris in 1887. The photograph taken by Frederick H. Evans in 1896 shows the room decorated with wall paper and fabric originally made by Thomas Clarkson (Bannister Hall) 'Small Stem' and 'Large Stem' and copied by Morris and Company. The same pattern is used for the chintz of the hangings of the early nineteenth-century mahogany four-poster bed in which Morris was born on 24 March 1834. On the bed there is the cushion cover, worked in satin stitch on green silk, designed and worked by May c. 1900, which won a prize at the Royal School of Needlework. On an English late seventeenth-century chest-of-drawers is Janey's jewel casket painted for her by Rossetti and his wife Elizabeth (Siddal). It is of high Gothic design, possibly by Webb, and so epitomises the inspiration of the Rossetti, Morris and Webb fraternity before 1862, the year of Lizzie Siddal's death.

The oil painting of Jane Morris is a copy made by Charles Fairfax-Murray in 1893 of Rossetti's Water-Willow portrait painted in 1871 at Kelmscott. The original painting is now in the Bancroft collection at the Delaware Art Museum, USA. The Manor and Kelmscott church appear in the

background. There is also a watercolour portrait of Jane Morris by C. M. Gere (1869-1957). By the bed hangs a small picture by May Morris herself of Naworth Castle, where William and Jane often stayed with the George and Rosalind Howard and their family (see p.20). By the door is a watercolour by T. M. Rooke, an employee of the Morris firm, of Philip Webb's study at 'Caxtons' near Worth in Sussex where Webb lived in his retirement from 1901 until his death in 1915. The cottage was rented from Wilfred Scawen Blunt. There are also two watercolours of 'Caudebec' and 'Dieppe' by T. M. Rooke, both dated September 1895. There is a small round oak table designed by Philip Webb, c. 1860, recorded as Mrs Morris's worktable at Red House. The

22
Mrs Morris's bedroom. Morris was born in the bed in 1834 at Walthamstow

carpet is a modern weaving of Lily 3-ply Kidderminster carpeting designed by Morris c. 1875.

WILLIAM MORRIS'S BEDROOM

Across the landing is Morris's bedroom. The walls are hung with 'Powdered' paper, a modern printing copying the paper in the Evans photo.

The most conspicuous object is Morris's early seventeenth-century oak four-poster bed. It was only from 1891 that it was decorated with the embroidered hangings that are now its most striking feature. In wools on natural coloured linen, they are beautiful examples of their kind and in remarkably fresh condition. The valance displays Morris's poem 'For the bed at Kelmscott', composed in 1891, embroidered by May Morris, helped, it is said, by Lily, sister of W. B. Yeats. The bed curtains too are by May. Their background pattern derives from the 1864 *Trellis* design with birds drawn by

23
Morris's bedroom and bed with embroideries by Jane and May Morris

Philip Webb, which was one of Morris's first for wallpaper. The bed spread with its naturalistic bouquets, delicate colouring and quotation from Morris's poem 'A Garden by the Sea' from the *Life and Death of Jason* (1867) was embroidered by Jane, who signed it 'Si je puis. Jane Morris. Kelmscott'. Framed beside the bed is the full-size design for the bed spread c. 1895.

The framed pictures above the fireplace are six of the set of fifteen woodblock prints and title-page of the *Apocalypse* by Albrecht Dürer (1471-1528). The woodcuts are from the 1498 edition and the title page from the 1511 edition. The young Morris and Burne Jones were drawn to the powerful images of Durer as early as their undergraduate days at Oxford. When Morris saw Durer's engraving of St Hubert in 1855 he wrote: 'What a splendid engraving that St Hubert is! O my word! so very, very gorgeous.'

24
Death-bed portrait of William Morris by Charles Fairfax-Murray

By the bookcase there is a most sensitive drawing of Morris on his death-bed. Charles Fairfax-Murray was with Morris when he died on 3rd October 1896 and straightaway drew four pencil drawings of him of which this is one. The whereabouts of the drawing were unknown until 1967 when an American, Ney Lannes MacMinn, resident on a barge moored in the Seine, bequeathed the pick of his Morris collection to Kelmscott Manor, and this drawing was one of the objects found in the barge.

The bookcase, designed by Webb, is from the library at Kelmscott House, Hammersmith, and contains a number of Morris's works and relevant books. Rossetti's pomegranate-and-lily design for a cushion cover and the completed cover worked from it, now much faded, flank the window. The carpet is a modern weaving of *Vine and Pomegranate* 3-ply Kidderminster-type carpeting designed by Morris or Kate Faulkner c. 1877.

By the entrance to the Tapestry Room are *Melancholia* by Albrecht Dürer (1471-1528) and two more engravings, *Bacchanal, with a wine press* by Andrea Mantegna (1431-1506) and *Allegory of the Power of love* by Cristofano Robetta (1462-c. 1522), both from Hammersmith. The depiction of the vines in the Mantegna may have inspired Morris's *Vine* design, since many of his acquisitions were made for inspirational purposes.

THE TAPESTRY ROOM

This has a stone fireplace with the Turner arms in sculpted relief, and tiles of *Persian Flower No.77* pattern available through the London retailer Thomas Elsley of the Portland metal works. The panelling is almost entirely hung with four of the series of mid seventeenth-century Brussels or Antwerp tapestries depicting the Life of Samson (Judges, 14-16): 'Feast in Timnath'; 'Samson and the smitten Philistines'; 'Delilah and Samson-blinded'; 'Samson and the pillars of the house'. They were here in 1871, and may have been here since the early eighteenth century.

25 *May Morris watercolour of The Tapestry Room*

The two pairs of *Peacock and Dragon* curtains are of the heavy compound-weave wool fabric designed by Morris in 1878. The German oil painting of Mathias Knutson aged 46, dated 1556, was left by Rossetti in 1874. The writing desk inlaid with bone is from Morris's study at Hammersmith and on it is Rossetti's paint box. In the centre is a rectangular table with turned legs. The black adjustable armchair is an example of one of the most popular Morris and Co. products, much plagiarised in America and known there as the 'Morris Chair'. The two brass Persian peacocks were at Kelmscott House, and they are mentioned by May Morris in her nostalgic description of the living room – 'opposite the fireplace stood the great Italian cypress-wood chest and thereon, with several pieces of oriental metal work, a pair of lordly peacocks of carven brass with jewelled necks, like guardians of a secret treasure. That side of the room had more than a touch of the Thousand and One Nights, for above this table of Eastern riches rose up a carpet spread like a canopy across the ceiling.'

26
The Tapestry Room

ATTICS

A steep split staircase, created in 1968, leads to the Attics. Morris described these attics in *News from Nowhere* (1890), as 'quaint garrets amongst the great timbers of the roof, where of old time the tillers and herdsmen of the manor slept, but which a-nights seemed now, by the small size of the beds, and the litter of useless and disregarded matters – bunches of dying flowers, feathers of birds, shells of starlings' eggs, caddis worms in mugs, and the like – to be inhabited for the time by children'.

In the West attic is a large hand-knotted carpet of the 'Bullerswood' design, originally woven about 1889 at the Merton Abbey works of Morris and Co. and probably designed by Morris and J. H. Dearle in collaboration. The original carpet was made for the Sanderson family for their house in Bullerswood. This example is on loan from Bath City Council.

In the great North Attic hangs the *Sunflower* embroidered hanging worked for Red House c. 1860. Like the *Daisy* hangings in the North Hall, it too is in laid and couched stitching in wools on a woollen ground. Sixteen tiles painted in glaze with the Judgement of Paris in a blue surround were probably designed by Burne-Jones. Among three pieces of Icelandic woodwork are the casket that was presented to May Morris who, with Miss

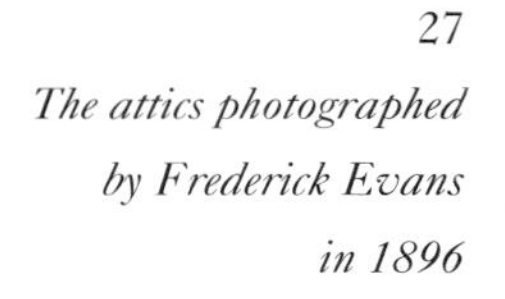
27
The attics photographed by Frederick Evans in 1896

Lobb, visited Iceland in the tracks of her father after the 1914-1918 war. The casket was carved by Rikardur Johnsson, and translated, the inscription on it reads 'For Morris-daughter. This small token of friendship tenders the thanks of Icelanders for your visit over the wide sea. May good fairies make your homeward journey safe', a sentiment which Morris would have appreciated.

In the garrets are some of the pieces of green-painted (originally green-stained) furniture, dressing tables, washstands, and towel horses, designed in the early years of the Morris firm by Ford Madox Brown between 1861 and 1875. They are unusual survivals. A contemporary wrote of Madox Brown, 'the furniture that he designed for himself was all so simple that it would not have been out of place in a working man's dwelling ... As far as he was concerned, he was socialist enough in theory and practice to consider that what was good enough for an artisan's house was fit for his own'. There are two mirrors designed by Philip Webb for Morris, Marshall, Faulkner and Company in the early 1860s.

28
Ford Madox Brown furniture 1861-1875

In the great South Attic, above the Old Hall, is a framed oil painting of 'Venus', possibly a design by Morris for one of the embroidered hangings for the dining room at Red House, c. 1860. There is also a lecture drop, which was a visual aid used by William Morris for a lecture on design.

On the tables is a collection of original textile samples from the firm, some unique and many with their identification and price labels still attached. Most were acquired from Albert Earl, an employee of Morris and Co. for a decade or more from about 1918.

At the south end, the 'Redcar' carpet was designed by Morris between c. 1881 for Sir Hugh Bell's house 'Red Barns' at Coatham, near Redcar, Yorkshire. The table case contains objects and books associated with William Morris including the Kelmscott Press edition of News from Nowhere and the 1958 facsimile of the Kelmscott Chaucer.

The brass rubbing is by William Morris of a memorial brass in Great Coxwell church commemorating one 'William Morys sumtyme fermer of Cokyswell' and Johane his wife c. 1510.

V TEXTILES

The textiles at the Manor fall into a number of groups. These are the tapestries that already existed in the house when Morris discovered it, the embroideries pre Red House, the embroideries associated with Red House, some products of the Morris's company, and the embroideries of May Morris.

TAPESTRIES IN TAPESTRY ROOM

These mid seventeenth-century Antwerp or Brussels tapestries were in the Manor in 1871. Morris's description reveals his interest in faded colours:

> 'The walls... are hung with tapestry of about 1600 representing the story of Sampson – they were never great works of art, and now when all the bright colours are faded out and nothing is left but the indigo blues, and greys and the warm yellow browns, they look better, I think, than they were meant to look; at any rate they make the walls a very pleasant background for the living people who haunt the room and in spite of the designer they give an air of romance which nothing else would quite do.'

The scenes from the life of Samson are taken from the Bible (Judges, 14-16) and include : Samson slaying the Lion (on the stairs); 'Feast in Timnath'; 'Samson and the smitten Philistines'; 'Delilah and Samson-blinded'; 'Samson and the pillars of the house'.

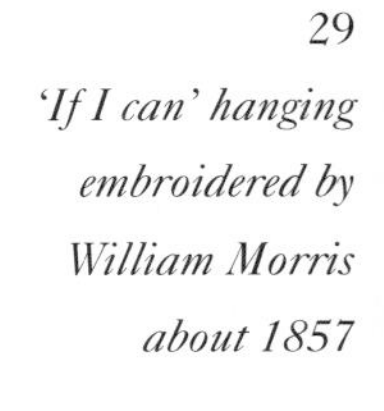

29
'If I can' hanging embroidered by William Morris about 1857

BEFORE RED HOUSE

30
Blue serge hanging from Red House. The daisy pattern was adapted by Morris from a fifteenth-century Froissart MS. and embroidered by Jane and friends and family

IF I CAN. This, the only known embroidery to have been worked by William Morris alone, was created at Red Lion Square in 1857. It shows a repeated design of birds and fruit trees surrounded by the motto +If+I+can+. It is on a linen ground embroidered with natural dyed wools in unorthodox flat and padded stitches. The irregular long and short stitches randomly placed form a stiff woollen cloth of similar texture and weight to woven tapestry. The design has a charming naivety enhanced by its faded colours and stylized birds. The pattern of repeating fruit trees with birds in flight is taken from Froissart's chronicle 'Dance of the Wodewoses' (BL Harley MS 4380, fol. 1 verso). The motto 'If I can' is taken from Van Eyck's motto *'als ich kanne'* normally written in Greek characters, which Morris used in designs freely translated as 'If I can' or *'si je puis'*, after his trip to the Low Countries in 1856.

RED HOUSE

Red House was designed by Philip Webb in 1859 for William Morris who had married Jane Burden that April. It was their home from 1860 to 1865. For the furnishing of the house Morris designed two schemes to be worked in embroidery; a set of panels for the drawing room depicting female figures and some curtains with repeating designs for the principal bedroom.

The curtains were made of dyed indigo blue woollen cloth, known as serge, and have rows of daisy clumps in laid and couched wool stitching, designed by William and embroidered by Janey Morris, her sister Bessie and Jane Faulkner, in yellow, red, and white wool. The design is derived from the manuscript of the Froissart chronicle noted above and was repeated later on tiles and on the Daisy wallpaper, the first Morris wallpaper to go into commercial production in 1863-4.

The panels, possibly either for the drawing room or dining room, were more adventurous and original in design but may never have been completed. The eight existing panels thought to be part of this scheme all depict famous historical women and were originally divided from each other by fruit and other trees. Three survive at Kelmscott and are identified as St. Catherine, Guenevere, and Penelope. They were designed to be embroidered onto plain linen, cut out and applied to a background in much the same way as late medieval embroideries. St Catherine, the only panel here to retain its tree, although there is another tree, unfinished, in the Victoria and Albert Museum, has been applied to velvet later in the form of a curtain whereas the other two are exhibited in their unfinished state. Penelope may be on the original green serge. Guenevere is unfinished and reveals the working technique.

31
St Catherine. Embroidered hanging worked by Jane Morris for Red House

SUNFLOWER. Decorative and signifying Constancy, sunflowers appear in Morris's painting on the walls of the Oxford Union. This embroidered hanging of repeating sunflowers, placed in a diagonal meander pattern, was probably made for Red House c. 1860. The embroidery is in yarns of green-dyed wool laid and couched on serge as the blue Daisy curtains. This embroidery in its boldness, uncompromising diagonal composition and sombre colours is one of the most startling and effective of Morris's early creations.

TAPESTRIES

CABBAGE AND VINE. This was William Morris's first tapestry woven by him at Kelmscott House between 10th May and 17th September 1879. His design and cartoon for it is in the Victoria and Albert Museum, and also his diary recording that it took 516 working hours, it was finished on 17th September. Morris wove in the traditional manner so that the weft is vertical when the tapestry is hung. As he was not used to wearing, the tension went wrong and created distortion. Called Acanthus and Vine, it was nicknamed Cabbage and Vine because of the leaves' unruliness. The design of this tapestry, which owes a great deal to the verdure panels (showing scenes of natural greenery with animals) seen in boyhood, uses the mirror repeating device of contemporary carpets and embroideries and depicts facing birds and swirling acanthus leaves.

The continuation of the production of tapestry by Morris and Co is shown by the *Millefleurs* tapestries in the Lobby to the Panelled Room (for which the tapestry designs are also shown) and in the Attic.

CURTAINS, HANGINGS AND CARPETS

In the stable barn hang a pair of thirteen-foot long Peacock and Dragon curtains designed by William Morris in 1878. These are of woollen twill jacquard handloom woven first at Queen Square and after 1881 at Merton Abbey. These curtains were originally used on the landing windows of the parental home of Dame Joan Evans, President of the Society of Antiquaries (1959-1964). It is unlikely that there were any carpets in the house in Morris's day. There are now two original Morris carpets Bullerswood and Redcar in the attics, which are shown so that they can be seen but not walked on. Many of the rest such as Lily in Jane Morris's bedroom and Vine and Pomegranate in William Morris's bedroom are modern copies, which were given to the Manor by J. R. Burrows of Boston USA.

32
The 'Cabbage and Vine' tapestry designed and woven by Morris in 1879

MAY MORRIS EMBROIDERY

May Morris did perhaps more than any other woman of her generation to elevate the status of embroidery as an art form. She was a superb technician and translator of designs. She became head of the Embroidery Department of Morris and Co in 1885, and much of the success of the Company's embroidery must be attributed to her work. By adopting a conscious 'design' approach to embroidery, she elevated its status from a domestic pastime to a serious art form. Her main work at the Manor is the valance and the curtains on Morris's bed. Slightly later is her prize winning cushion cover on the bed in Jane Morris's bedroom. She also embroidered the tablemats in the Hall and the 1920s embroidered panel in the Screens Passage.

MORRIS'S BED. It was only from 1891 that the bed was decorated with the embroidered hangings in wools on natural coloured linen that are now its most striking feature. The vallance displays Morris's poem 'For the bed at Kelmscott', composed in 1891, embroidered by May Morris, helped, it is said, by Lily, sister of W. B. Yeats.

The wind's on the wold and the night is a-cold
And Thames runs chill twixt' mead and hill,
But kind and dear is the old house here
And my heart is warm midst winter's harm.
Rest then and rest, and think of the best
Twixt summer and spring when all birds sing
In the town of the tree and ye lie in me
And scarce dare move lest earth and its love
Should fade away ere the full of the day.

I am old and have seen many things that have been,
Both grief and peace and wane and increase.
No tale I tell of ill or well
But this I say night treadeth on day
And for worst and best right good is rest.

The curtains are by May and their background pattern derives from the 1864 Trellis design with birds drawn by Philip Webb, which was one of Morris's first for wallpaper. Framed beside the bed is the full-size design for the bedspread. This with its naturalistic bouquets, delicate colouring and quotation from Morris's poem 'A Garden by the Sea' from the Life and Death of Jason (1867) was embroidered by Mrs. Morris, who signed it 'Si je puis. Jane Morris. Kelmscott'.

33

Morris's bed curtains, (detail). Embroidered by May Morris and helpers, 1891-1894

VI GARDEN

The best account of the way Morris perceived the gardens at Kelmscott is the descriptions of the approach to the house at the end of the journey in *News from Nowhere* and in the essay called 'Gossip about an Old House on the Upper Thames' that has already been quoted (see p.1).

34
Morris in the Home Mead. Carving by George Jack, from a sketch by Philip Webb, on the 'Memorial Cottages' built in Kelmscott village in 1902

The gardens at Kelmscott may be divided into the historic gardens around the house and the West Meadow. The blight of Dutch elm disease has meant that the high elm trees which gave the house its secluded air in Morris's day are unlikely to regenerate. An attempt to recreate something of the atmosphere of the gardens as they were in Morris's time began in 1993. The work was directed by Hal Moggridge and Stephanie Carter of Colvin and Moggridge. It has been aided by grants from the Carnegie Foundation and other individuals and bodies.

FRONT GARDEN

Here the aim is to recreate the appearance recorded in the drawing by Charles Gere of the East front (pl. 1). Standard roses (including Mary Rose, Heritage, Sir Edward Elgar and Countryman) have been planted to either side of the path. There is a very fine weeping ash here, and the summer house with its wicker-work sides was present by the 1880s. In the time of William Morris the yew hedge on the north side was shaped in the form of a dragon, which he called Fafnir. The hedge is in the process of being recut to its original shape, under the direction of Philip Cotton, formerly head gardener at Cliveden. Until it is finished the hedge may look rather ugly.

THE NORTH AND WEST OF THE HOUSE

Vegetable gardens can be seen in the E. H. New drawing (pl 4). A rough-hewn pergola, planted with roses and vines, leads from the north door of the Manor to the door in the north wall of the garden. To the north west of the house there was an orchard, which was recreated in 1995 and is now planted with old apple trees (Blenheim Orange, Gascoyne's Scarlet, Lady Sudeley, King of the

35
The west garden in spring

Pippins, Adam's Pearmain, American Mother, and Beauty of Bath). To the west of the house there is a fine old mulberry tree. Around this tree paths and flowerbeds have been created. The orchard is divided from the flowerbeds by a rustic pole fence with roses along it. All these features reproduce the appearance indicated by photos taken in May Morris's day.

THE FARMYARD

The farmyard was not leased by Morris and was owned by the Church Commissioners until after the Manor had been acquired by the Society of Antiquaries. The buildings consist of the South Road barn, which since 1996 has housed an exhibition relating the history of the house, the Tea Room barn, the detached Dovecote, and the Brick barn, that now serves as a shop. At the back of this, there is a lean-to with yard partly bounded by fine stone slabs set vertically and stone troughs. Most of the roofs have fine Stonesfield slates, a feature that drew Morris to the Manor.

THE WEST MEADOW

It was in this meadow that George Jack portrayed Morris in the carving on the Memorial Cottages. It is now being managed as a meadow with appropriate traditional trees such as Crab Apples, Ash, Willow, Walnut, Black Poplar and Horse Chestnut.

VII VILLAGE

The road from the river leads, past the 'door in the wall', to Kelmscott village. A much more detailed guide to the village is being produced as part of the work of the Kelmscott Landscape Survey. The fence adjacent to the road on the left is made of large flat stone slabs set vertically in the ground with iron restraining posts and ties where necessary. This was created by Gimson at the same time as he designed the pair of cottages which were built for May Morris in memory of Jane. Ernest Gimson (1864-1919) designed them in 1914. They contain 'simple but admirable joinery'.

THE MEMORIAL COTTAGES

The two loftier semi-detached cottages were designed by Philip Webb and built for Jane Morris in 1902 as a memorial to Morris; the stone sculpture on the front shows Morris sitting in the home mead west of the Manor was carved by George Jack from a sketch by Webb.

THE MORRIS MEMORIAL HALL

The village hall, west of the road leading from the Plough Inn to the church, was also designed by Ernest Gimson. May Morris asked him to design it not long after he had produced the designs for the two cottages and she was largely instrumental in raising the money for its completion in 1934, when it was opened on 20th October by George Bernard Shaw.

THE CHURCH

36
The exterior of St George's church seen from the south west

At the north end of the village stands the parish church of St George. In the south-east part of the churchyard is the grave of William, Jane, Jenny and May Morris marked by a great coped stone designed initially for William Morris by his old friend and partner Philip Webb; a bill for £25 8s. 6d., from Lawrence Turner for carving and setting it, was certified by Webb on 1 June 1898. Impressive in its simplicity, the decoration on the stone already evinces the arts and crafts style, and the inscriptions added for each member of the family are fine examples of lettering, though none perhaps attains to the beauty of the original for William himself. 'You see', wrote Webb to Janey in 1897, 'I have made it rudely simple, dividing the slopes of the roof into the required four spaces with a slip of tree on both sides, which seem to represent to me his own hands from the words of himself in the November prologue in the *Earthly Paradise*.

> "In whose void patience how can these have part
> These outstretched feverish hands, this restless heart?"

37
Philip Webb's design for William Morris's tombstone in St George's Churchyard at Kelmscott

VIII EPILOGUE THE SOCIETY OF ANTIQUARIES AND KELMSCOTT

William Morris was elected a Fellow of the Society in 1896. He was impressed by the continuity of the Society. Jane died in 1913 and left the manor to their daughter May. May made her will in 1929 and named the Society as the residuary legatee. Her sister Jenny died in 1935 and left her residuary estate to the Society to form a Fund known as the William and Jane Morris Fund. This still exists and gives grants to churches and other monuments.

38

William Morris's overcoat

May remained in possession of the Manor until her death in 1938 when, under the terms of her will, the property went in trust to the University of Oxford. Nearly a quarter of a century later, on 4 January 1962, the trust was declared invalid in the High Court and, in consequence, Kelmscott passed to the Society of Antiquaries as the residuary legatee of the Morris estate.

In 1962 the Society was not well endowed and there was no money for the necessary restoration. The immediate reaction was to sell it. However, Joan Evans, the President at the time, dined with her niece Susan Minet. She was related to William Minet, Treasurer of the Society from 1913 to 1933. Sitting by the fire after dinner, doing their Morris embroidery, Joan Evans said 'We have just inherited a beautiful and interesting house, which we cannot afford to keep.' A week later, a letter arrived from a firm of solicitors carrying Miss Minet's wish to give the Society shares in the Globe Insurance Company which had been purchased in the late eighteenth century. The value in 1962 was £350,000, of which the Society used £40,000 to do up the Manor, and the rest went into the General Fund of the Society. Kelmscott Manor was the cause of this substantial bequest to the Society.

The restoration was carried out by Donald Insall and Associates, and Peter Locke was the architect in sole charge of the undertaking. The main addition made at this time was the north porch added in 1966. It was the enthusiasm of Dr. A. R. Dufty, Secretary of the Society at the time of the legal judgement, which ensured that the manor was restored. He died in 1993, and it is a fitting memorial to him to note how much the public owes to his foresight. It was his determination and vision that encouraged the Society to take on Kelmscott Manor in the belief that the rehabilitation of an ancient house and the preservation of its remarkable contents were excellent aims. It is the policy of the Society today to welcome many visitors from all over the world and to continue to do all it can to preserve and make available to as many as possible this remarkable treasure.

FURTHER READING

William Morris, A life for our time by Fiona MacCarthy, London 1994.

Jane and May Morris, a biographical story 1839-1938 by Jan Marsh, London 1986.

William Morris: Art and Kelmscott edited by Linda Parry, Antiquaries Occasional Paper London 1996. This includes the article by A. R. Dufty, 'William Morris and the Kelmscott Estate' Antiquaries Journal, 43 (1963), part 1.

William Morris edited by Linda Parry 1996. Catalogue of the exhibition 'William Morris 1834-1896' at the Victoria and Albert Museum, London.

William Morris and Kelmscott Design Council in association with the West Surrey College of Art and Design, Farnham 1981.

David Pendery 'Ernest Gimson's Work in Kelmscott' *Journal of the William Morris Society* vol X, no. 3, Autumn 1993.

Morris Embroideries, The Prototypes by A. R. Dufty, London 1985.

William Morris Textiles by Linda Parry, London 1983.

The Church of St. George Kelmscott by A. R. Dufty Leopard's Head Press, 1991.

May Morris 1862-1938 William Morris Gallery, Walthamstow 1989.

Dante Gabriel Rossetti Catalogue edited by Julian Treuherz, Elizabeth Prettejohn and Edwin Becker. Zwolle and Liverpool. 2003. Catalogue of the exhibition held at the Walker Liverpool and the Van Gogh Museum, Amsterdam 2003-4.